Famous Female
Authors

J.K. ROWLING

Author of the
HARRY POTTER SERIES

by Jennifer Hunsicker

CAPSTONE PRESS
a capstone imprint

Snap Books are published by Capstone Press,
1710 Roe Crest Drive, North Mankato, Minnesota 56003
www.mycapstone.com

Library of Congress Cataloging-in-Publication Data
Cataloging-in-Publication Data is on file with the Library of Congress.
978-1-5157-1328-9 (library binding)
978-1-5157-1336-4 (paperback)
978-1-5157-1340-1 (eBook PDF)

Editorial Credits
Abby Colich, editor; Bobbi J. Wyss, designer;
Kelly Garvin, media researcher; Laura Manthe, production specialist

Photo Credits
Alamy: Ben Molyneux, 22, Tim Graham, 21, VIEW Pictures Ltd. 9; Newscom: Andy
Rain/EPA, 29, David Fisher/REX, 25, exen/Splash News, 27, Marius Alexander/REX,
19(bottom), REX, 15, Seamus Murphy/REX, 5; Shutterstock: 89studio, 7, 20, Everett
Collection, 6, Ivica Drusany, 19 (t), Mikadum, 16, Peartree, cover (b), 1, Robert
Neumann, 11, Sean Pavone, 13, Tursunbaev Ruslan, cover, 1

Printed in China.
007736

TABLE OF CONTENTS

CHAPTER 1

Harry Potter Fever

The police held back a screaming mob. Some people were even crying. Camera lights flashed. A line of people snaked through the streets. They were attempting to get onto Platform 9 $\frac{3}{4}$ at King's Cross Station in London. Fans and members of the press boarded a steam train disguised as Hogwart's Express. Author J.K. Rowling waved out the window to the hundreds who couldn't get on. Steam rose from the red train as it chugged away.

A WORLD OF WIZARDRY

It was July 8, 2000. J.K. Rowling's **publisher** was promoting the release of *Harry Potter and the Goblet of Fire*. This book was the fourth in the blockbuster Harry Potter series.

The frenzy around Harry Potter's world had grown since the first book's release in 1997. Fans wanted to know more. What would happen to Harry, Hermione, and Ron? How would the **series**—that would take 17 years of Jo Rowling's life to write—end? How did this wizard world even begin? It started with imagination. It grew from a writer's life full of challenges.

publisher—a company that makes and sells printed things, such as newspapers or books

series—a number of things coming one after another

Jo Rowling on the train at King's Cross Station in 2000

CHAPTER 2

Meet Jo

Joanne Rowling was born July 31, 1965, in Yate, England. In keeping with family tradition, Jo, as she became known, did not have a middle name. Almost two years later, Joanne's younger sister, Di, was born.

Anne and Pete, Jo's parents, filled their home with love, books, and music. They played their favorite Beatles records and danced around the living room. Anne played the guitar. Both parents encouraged reading. Anne kept shelves full of books for herself and her children. She frequently read to her daughters.

Jo Rowling

CHILDHOOD CHEER AND CHALLENGE

Young Jo was a dreamer. She wrote her first story, "Rabbit," at age 6. She made up stories and games with wizards, witches, and all kinds of forest folk. She, her sister, and the neighborhood children brought Jo's stories to life. They acted them out in the nearby woods.

When Jo was 15, doctors diagnosed her mother with multiple sclerosis (MS). This was not an easy time for the Rowling family, but life went on. Jo attended high school. She became interested in global **social justice** issues. She was very concerned about the evils and inequality that other people endured throughout the world.

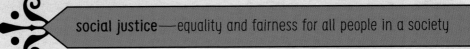

social justice—equality and fairness for all people in a society

MULTIPLE SCLEROSIS

MS is a crippling disease. It causes weakness and a loss of feeling in the limbs. Vision loss can also occur. Anne was not able to do the things she once loved, including playing the guitar. As the disease progressed, she needed extra help for things most people can do with ease, such as walking.

CHAPTER 3

College and Work

Beginning in 1983 Jo attended Exeter University in England. Interested in a future as a writer, Jo wanted to study English literature. Her parents, however, encouraged her to study modern languages. They thought modern languages would help her find a good job after graduating.

Jo compromised. She studied both French and the Classics. Studying French pleased her parents. Classics let her study the **mythology** she loved. It also fed her desire to become a writer.

ALWAYS A STORYTELLER

Jo frequently went out with her friends for fun. She studied enough to get by as an average student. She remained a storyteller in everything she did. When her friends talked about their problems, Jo turned the tales of woe into spy stories. Her friends found this entertaining.

mythology—the study of stories or beliefs of untrue beings, such as gods or heroes, of a particular people

> " I was striking an uneasy balance between the ambition I had for myself, and what those closest to me expected of me. "
>
> —Jo Rowling, Harvard University Commencement Speech, June 5, 2008

Exeter University

LIFE IN LONDON

Jo graduated from Exeter University in 1986. Her mother watched the ceremony from the audience in a wheelchair. Jo soon moved to London. She found a job with Amnesty International. Here she researched human rights issues against French-speaking people in Africa. She spent her lunch and free time writing fiction.

In 1990, during a train ride between Manchester and London, Jo dreamily looked out the window. In her mind she saw a sad little boy on a train going to a school for wizards. Jo perked up. No paper. No pencil. She settled down with her imagination. Her mind wandered. Jo began building the little boy's world with characters and scenes. She knew she had a story. This was the day she met Harry Potter, a character who's been with her ever since.

✔ FACT

Amnesty International is a **nonprofit** organization. It works to protect people from human rights violations. They fight against **poverty**, violence, and other abuses.

nonprofit—not existing to make money
poverty—the state of being poor or without money

The idea for Harry Potter came to Jo while she was riding a train. The Hogwart's Express train would become an important part of the Harry Potter story. Parts of the movie were filmed over the Glenfinnan Viaduct in Scotland.

LOSING HER MOTHER

After a 10-year battle with MS, Jo's mother died. It was New Year's Eve, 1990. Anne was 45 years old. Though Jo didn't realize it at the time, she expressed her grief through her writing. Much of Harry Potter includes references to her mother. For example, Harry's greatest wish was to see his parents who had died. Jo's greatest wish was to see her mother again.

Jo had never been able to hold down a job for very long. She always seemed different from her coworkers. They socialized during lunch. Jo spent the time writing. Soon after her mother's death, Jo knew she needed a change.

In 1991 Jo got a position teaching English in Porto, Portugal's second largest city. On weeknights and Saturday mornings, she taught. During the day Jo sat in the many cafés around town. She spent this time writing about Harry Potter and his wizarding world.

Porto, Portugal

CHAPTER 4

Marriage and Baby

Jo and her friends often spent time out and about in Porto. One evening at a **disco**, Jo met Jorge Arantes, a journalism student. They fell in love. Jo and Jorge had a bumpy relationship. They argued a lot, but they loved each other. On October 16, 1992, they got married.

LEAVING JORGE

Jo gave birth to her daughter Jessica on July 27, 1993. Jo and Jorge continued to clash. During one of their fights, Jorge dragged Jo out of their home and into the street. She screamed at him. He slammed the door in her face and locked it behind him. Scared and separated from her 4-month-old daughter, Jo asked a friend for help. They called the police. Jo quickly got the baby and left. She knew she could never return.

disco—a dance club or place where people dance

Jo, Jorge, and Jessica in 1993

Edinburgh, Scotland

> I had failed on an epic scale. An exceptionally short-lived marriage had imploded, and I was jobless, a lone parent, and as poor as it is possible to be in modern Britain, without being homeless.

—Jo Rowling, Harvard University Commencement Speech, June 5, 2008

MOVING TO SCOTLAND

Jo took Jessica and left for Edinburgh, Scotland. They stayed with her sister, Di, and Di's husband. Jo told Di about Harry Potter for the first time. She let her read the first three chapters. Di encouraged Jo to write more.

After the move Jo had no job and a baby to care for. She and baby Jessica moved into one of the only apartments Jo could afford. It had no heat. Mice were everywhere. To make matters worse, Jo had to apply for financial help from the government. The money still wasn't enough to cover expenses. Jo swallowed her pride and borrowed money from a friend. Eventually, she found a better apartment. She lived there with Jessica for the next three years. Times were not easy. They could only afford the bare minimum, but it was home.

Jo had never wanted to admit to anyone how afraid she was of Jorge's temper. But when he came to Edinburgh looking for her, she got a **restraining order** against him. Jorge went back to Porto. Jo filed for divorce.

restraining order—an issue from a court intended to help protect a victim of violence or threats

CHAPTER 5

Challenges and Dreams

Jo had no job. Her only income was the money from the government. Jo became depressed. She cried because she could not provide for her child the way she wanted to. Other children around her seemed to have so many toys. Jessica's toys were so few. But having a daughter gave her the courage to seek help. Jo went to counselling.

CONTINUING TO WRITE

Jo knew she could not change her circumstances quickly. She spent time writing her book until she figured out what to do next. She knew she might never again have a chance to dedicate so much time to writing. Every day she put Jessica in her stroller. They walked until Jessica went to sleep. Jo would then go to a café, drink coffee, and write. The story of Harry Potter continued to grow.

✔ FACT

Jo wrote family histories for all of the Harry Potter characters. She knows so much more about the world she has created than will ever appear in her books.

Jo wrote much of the first Harry Potter book at *The Elephant House* in Edinburgh.

A SMASH HIT

How was Jo going to break out of poverty? She continued to write. Jo finished the first Harry Potter book in 1995.

After finishing the book, Jo decided she wanted to become a teacher. But first she needed a teaching certificate. Jo started a yearlong post-graduate program in education.

This same year Jo's divorce from Jorge became final. Things were looking up.

While waiting to begin teaching, Jo searched for an **agent**. She sent out several **queries**. The agent Christopher Little agreed to represent her. He did not usually do children's stories, but he believed in Harry Potter. Christopher Little sent the book out to 13 publishers. All rejected it, except for one—Bloomsbury. Her book would be published! Jo danced around the kitchen table when she found out. Bloomsbury paid her an **advance** of £1,500 (about $2,400). With the money Jo and Jessica moved into a better apartment.

PEN NAMES

Jo's publisher asked her to use initials instead of her real name. They thought boys might not read a book by a woman. She chose the initial K in honor of her grandmother Kathleen. She had her first pen name, J.K. Rowling. Jo uses other pen names too. Her other *pseudonyms* include Newt Scamander, Kennilworthy Whisp, and Robert Galbraith.

Jo in her publisher Bloomsbury's office in London

agent—someone who helps a writer find a publisher

query—a letter sent asking for information or a response

advance—a payment given prior to work being completed

pseudonym—a fictitious name

BOOK RELEASES

Jo's publishers told her she wouldn't make much money writing children's books. So she followed through on her plans. Jo got a job teaching French. She also applied for and received a **grant** to work on the next Harry Potter book.

In 1997 Great Britain saw the release of *Harry Potter and the Philosopher's Stone*. Scholastic bought the rights to publish the book in the United States. The U.S. release came the following year. Scholastic gave the book a different title, *Harry Potter and the Sorcerer's Stone*. The U.S. publishers thought kids wouldn't want to read a book with the word "philosopher" in the title.

books in the Harry Potter series with covers produced by Bloomsbury in the United Kingdom

SOARING SUCCESS

Jo had to wait months for her first **royalty** payment. It was small. Jo kept teaching.

But soon *Harry Potter and the Sorcerer's Stone* soared to the top of *The New York Times* Best Sellers list. *Harry Potter and the Chamber of Secrets*, published the following year, made the list as well. Jo's royalty checks got bigger. The third book, *Harry Potter and the Prisoner of Azkaban*, came out in 1999. Soon the Harry Potter books held the top three slots on the Best Sellers list. This was unheard of for children's books at the time. Jo Rowling would never experience poverty again.

✔ FACT

Normally, only adult hardcover books made the top of *The New York Times* Best Sellers list. After the success of the Harry Potter books, the newspaper decided to create separate lists. There are now lists for adult books and children's books.

grant—a gift such as land or money given for a particular purpose
royalty—a payment from a share in a profit

Success and What to Do with It

Jo's fourth book, *Harry Potter and the Goblet of Fire*, was released in 2000. It was the first in the series released on the same day in the United States and the United Kingdom. More than 5 million copies were printed. Jo rode the Hogwart's Express with fans, media, and her publishers to celebrate the launch of the book.

A BREAK FROM WRITING

By this time Jo had published four books in four years. So much had happened so quickly. Jo was having trouble writing. This had never happened to her before. She knew she needed to take a break. Her publishers understood.

During this break, Jo fell in love again. On December 26, 2001, she married Dr. Neil Murray. They had two children together. David was born in 2003. Mackenzie was born in 2005.

Jo published the final three books in the Harry Potter series between 2003 and 2007. With more than 450 million copies printed worldwide, Harry Potter is the highest-selling series in history.

Jo and her husband, Neil

> " From about 2000, I knew there would never be any topping Harry Potter. My publishers had got this train for the book launch... I looked out at all the people screaming ... I remember thinking, 'You will never top this.' [Now] I can say, 'Oh, I will never top it,' or I can see how lucky I am.

—Jo Rowling, Independent Bath Literature Festival, March 10, 2013 "

CHOOSING CHARITIES

Jo continues to earn money from Harry Potter and her other projects. *Forbes* magazine first listed her as one of the world's billionaires in 2004. Since then Jo has given away hundreds of millions of dollars. She no longer makes the billionaire list.

Jo donates to many causes that are important to her. In 2005 she began her own charity, Lumos. Lumos works to help children in orphanages around the world.

Having known the hardships of being a single parent, Jo also supports the National Council for One Parent Families. Jo uses her best weapon, her pen, to write articles educating the public on the realities of single-parent families.

Jo also supports research for the treatment of MS. In remembrance of her mother, Jo opened the Anne Rowling Neurology Clinic in 2013.

Also, Jo wrote *Fantastic Beasts and Where to Find Them* and *Quidditch Through the Ages*, two Harry Potter textbooks. She donated the proceeds to the charity Comic Relief.

✔ FACT

Comic Relief is a charity based in the United Kingdom. Its goal is "a just world, free from poverty."

Jo at an event to raise money for Lumos

CHAPTER 7

Other Projects

Jo may be a writer first, but her imagination is also suited for the digital world. In 2011 she partnered with Sony. Together they developed Pottermore, a website for her fans. Jo worked with Sony again to create PlayStation 3's Wonderbook software. She wrote content for the Wonderbook games The Book of Spells and The Book of Potions.

HARRY POTTER AND MORE

Jo continues to write about the wizarding world. The play *Harry Potter and the Cursed Child* opened in London in 2016. It is considered the eighth installment in the Harry Potter series.

Jo wrote her first **screenplay** based on *Fantastic Beasts and Where to Find Them*. The film is the first in a trilogy that is set before the original Harry Potter series. The movie debuted in 2016.

Outside of Harry Potter, Jo has written *The Casual Vacancy*. Released in 2012, the book is geared toward adults. As Robert Galbraith, she also penned the three-book Cormoran Strike series.

Whether it's more Harry Potter or new books for adults, the world can be assured Jo will keep writing.

screenplay—the written version of a movie or TV show

> " I have so many ideas. I sometimes worry I'll die before I've written them all out ... that I will leave this earth without having written them all. "
>
> —Jo Rowling interview with Radio Times, November 2, 2015

Jo at a photo shoot to promote Pottermore

Glossary

advance (ad-VANSS)—a payment given prior to work being completed

agent (AY-juhnt)—someone who helps a writer find a publisher

disco (disk-COH)—a dance club or place where people dance

grant (GRANT)—a gift such as land or money given for a particular purpose

mythology (mith-AWL-uh-jee)—the study of stories or beliefs of untrue beings, such as gods or heroes, of a particular people

nonprofit (non-PROFF-ett)—not existing to make money

poverty (PAW-vuhr-tee)—the state of being poor or without money

pseudonym (SOOD-uh-nimm)—a fictitious name

publisher (PUHB-lish-er)—a company that makes and sells printed things, such as newspapers or books

query (KWARE-ee)—a letter sent asking for information or a response

restraining order (reh-STRANE-ing OR-dur)—an issue from a court intended to help protect a victim of violence or threats

royalty (ROI-uhl-tee)—a payment from a share in a profit

screenplay (SKREEN-play)—the written version of a movie or TV show

series (SIHR-eez)—a number of things coming one after another

social justice (SOH-shuhl JUHSS-tiss)—equality and fairness for all people in a society

Read More

Anderson, Jennifer Joline. *Writing Fantastic Fiction*. Write This Way. Minneapolis: Lerner Publications, 2016.

Bowman, Chris. *J.K. Rowling*. Blastoff! Readers: Children's Storytellers. Minneapolis: Bellwether Media, 2016.

Pezzi, Bryan. *J.K. Rowling*. Great Storytellers. New York: Smartbook Media, Inc., 2016.

Internet Sites

FactHound offers a safe, fun way to find Internet sites related to this book. All of the sites on FactHound have been researched by our staff.

Here's all you do:

Visit *www.facthound.com*

Type in this code: 9781515713289

Check out projects, games and lots more at
www.capstonekids.com

Critical Thinking Using the Common Core

1. When did Jo get the idea to write Harry Potter? (Key Idea and Details)

2. What if Jo had found a job that paid well after she moved to Scotland? Do you think she still would have finished writing the Harry Potter books? Explain why or why not. (Integration of Knowledge and Ideas)

3. Reread the text and caption on pages 26 and 27. What feelings do you think Jo had while the photo was being taken? (Craft and Structure)

Index